COUNTRIES OF THE WORLD

Russia

Gareth Stevens Publishing
MILWAUKEE

About the author: Terence M. G. Rice studied Russian language and literature at the London School of Slavonic and Eastern European Studies and at the Moscow State University. He has worked as a foreign language editor, translator, and free-lance interpreter. His extensive experience with Russia and Russians spans almost thirty years.

Written by
TERENCE M. G. RICE

Edited by
KAREN KWEK

Designed by
LYNN CHIN

Picture research by
SUSAN JANE MANUEL

First published in North America in 1999 by
Gareth Stevens Publishing
1555 North RiverCenter Drive, Suite 201
Milwaukee, Wisconsin 53212 USA

For a free color catalog describing
Gareth Stevens' list of high-quality books
and multimedia programs, call
1-800-542-2595 (USA) or
1-800-461-9120 (CANADA)
Gareth Stevens Publishing's
Fax: (414) 225-0377.
See our catalog, too, on the World Wide Web:
gsinc.com

© **TIMES EDITIONS PTE LTD 1999**
Originated and designed by
Times Books International
an imprint of Times Editions Pte Ltd
Times Centre, 1 New Industrial Road
Singapore 536196
http://www.timesone.com.sg/te

Library of Congress Cataloging-in-Publication Data
Rice, Terence M.G.
    Russia / [Rice, Terence M. G.].
    p.   cm. -- (Countries of the world)
    Includes bibliographical references and index.
    Summary: Surveys the history, geography, government, economy,
    culture, people, and foreign relations of Russia.
    ISBN 0-8368-2263-3 (lib. bdg.)
    1. Russia (Federation)--Juvenile literature. [1. Russia (Federation)]
    I. Title. II. Series: Countries of the world (Milwaukee, Wis.)
    DK510.23.R49   1999
    947--dc21   98-8858

Printed in Singapore

1 2 3 4 5 6 7 8 9 03 02 01 00 99

Contents

AN OVERVIEW OF RUSSIA

Russia is the largest country in the world, covering about one-eighth of Earth's landmass. Traveling by train across Russia is a major undertaking — it takes eight whole days to get from coast to coast! When the sun sets in Kaliningrad in the west, it is rising over Cape Dezhnev, the easternmost point of this vast country. Throughout history, from the arrival of the Vikings to communism and beyond, empires have left their mark on Russia. Periods of great progress and expansion have alternated with political instability and the hardships of war. Today, Russia is venturing into a market economy and rapidly modernizing, following the example of the West. It is also trying to preserve its traditions, while leaving behind the unhappy mistakes of the past.

Opposite: **Moscow is often represented by one of its most spectacular sights, the Church of Intercession on the Moat, also called St. Basil's Cathedral. Built in the sixteenth century, the cathedral consists of nine churches combined in one magnificent structure.**

Below: **Children are the hope, pride, and joy of the Russian people.**

THE FLAG OF RUSSIA

Russia, or the Russian Federation, consists of twenty-one republics, excluding Russia itself. When these regions were part of the Union of Soviet Socialist Republics (U.S.S.R.), they shared a flag featuring a hammer-and-sickle motif on a red background. The hammer and sickle represented revolution, and the color red, communism. In 1991, the U.S.S.R. dissolved. The present white-blue-red flag has been a state symbol of Russia since the late nineteenth century. Today, Russia and eleven other former Soviet republics cooperate loosely as the Commonwealth of Independent States (CIS).

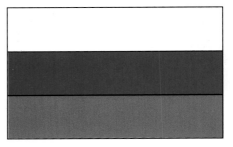

Geography

Diverse Landscapes

Covering an area of 6.6 million square miles (17.1 million square kilometers), Russia is almost twice as large as either the United States or China. It spans eleven time zones and supports a population of about one hundred and fifty million. The capital of the country is Moscow.

Russia's vast land area includes a diversity of landscapes. The far north lies within the Arctic Circle and consists of frozen plains. Stunted vegetation and mosses grow in the subarctic or tundra belt, and raging blizzards are common in winter. South of this belt lies the taiga, which consists of marshy pine forests. These give way to mixed forests of birch and pine in warmer regions. Moscow and St. Petersburg lie within this temperate belt. Farther south, the forests disappear, replaced by vast, fertile plains known as the steppe. The drainage basins of Russia's majestic rivers form its lowland plains. The Ob, Yenisey, and Lena rivers are among the longest in the world.

Below: **Near the Mongolian border, nestled in the midst of mountains, is one of the most beautiful lakes in the world, Lake Baykal. The Trans-Siberian Railway runs south of the lake, winding eastward to the Pacific port of Vladivostok.**

About 80 percent of the total population of Russia is concentrated in its western part. This flat region is interrupted only by some low hills called the Central Russian Upland. The great Volga and Don rivers begin here. The Baltic, Caspian, and Black seas flank the western coast of Russia. Great snow-capped mountains, the Caucasus, form the southern border. Towering at a majestic 18,510 feet (5,640 meters) is the highest of the Caucasus peaks, Mt. Elbrus. East of the western plain, the land rises to the Ural Mountains. Although not nearly as impressive as the Caucasus in height, they form the border between Europe and Asia, running from the Arctic, southward to the edge of Kazakhstan, which is largely desert.

Well-known as a freezing wilderness and land of exile, Siberia lies east of the Ural Mountains. Winters are so cold on the Central Siberian Plateau that if one digs into the ground in summer, when it does get hot, the soil is still frozen. This icy layer is known as permafrost. Eastern Russia is dominated by mountain ranges. In the southeast lies Kamchatka, while in the northeast, the Chukchi Peninsula points toward Alaska.

Above: **Hot gases and steam rise from a sulfur pool in Kamchatka, a peninsula in eastern Russia. Kamchatka has many geysers, hot springs, and active volcanoes. It lies on the Ring of Fire, the volcanic zone that encircles the Pacific Ocean.**

Long Winters and White Nights

Most people associate the Russian winter with snow and ice, earmuffs, and huge fur hats. In fact, it often gets very cold in winter. In western Russia, January temperatures average just below 32° Fahrenheit (0° Celsius). In the north and east, it gets as cold as -90° F (-68° C)! Winter conditions may be harsh, but the snow-covered landscape is often peaceful and beautiful.

Fortunately, Russia is not always cold. Spring comes quickly in April and May in the western parts of Russia, reaching the north and east a little later. The snow melts, and the flowers bud and bloom soon after. Hot summer days are frequently accompanied by short, violent thunderstorms. In the far north, above the Arctic Circle, the sun does not set for weeks at a stretch. Russians in St. Petersburg celebrate White Nights at this time of year. In the east, temperatures get quite warm during the short summer (June to September), but mosquitoes make life in the marshy land almost unbearable!

Autumn, with its brilliant colors, has always been the favorite season of Russian poets. The beauty of the season and its traditional associations with harvest have inspired many works of art. Later in the year, the rains come, the nights get longer, and winter begins its icy reign once again.

Above: **Autumn in the Russian countryside. In September, the days often remain warm, but the first frosts of the year arrive during autumn nights. The leaves change color, a spectacular sight for all who stroll by pursuing a popular national hobby — picking mushrooms.**

THE SIBERIAN TIGER

Few of these beautiful animals remain in the wild today, but protection and research may help save the species.
(*A Closer Look, page 66*)

Plants and Animals

The far north cannot support many plants, but mosses, lichens, and shrubs do grow. Herds of reindeer depend on this vegetation for food. Polar bears, walruses, seals, inland wolves, and arctic foxes often appear on the northern coasts.

Farther south, brown bears and smaller animals, such as mink, beavers, marmots, and weasels, are hunted for their fur. Silver birch trees grow in the south, along with a few hundred varieties of edible mushrooms. On the steppe, rare herds of saiga (a kind of antelope with a turned-down snout) graze in the spring, drawn by the prairie flowers and the Caspian Sea.

Siberia's plants and animals are similar to those found in western Russia. There are, however, some surprises, such as the Siberian tiger, the largest member of the cat family. Sadly, the Siberian tiger is now endangered. Lake Baykal has over a thousand species of animals found only there — including a freshwater seal (the nerpa) and some very strange-looking fish.

THE BROWN BEAR

A favorite Russian mascot, this animal is admired for its strength and courage.

(A Closer Look, page 44)

Left: **Herds of deer are slowly losing their natural habitat to deforestation and industrialization.**

9

History

The Vikings Arrive

By the ninth century, Slav tribes were living in the forests of what is now Ukraine, fighting among themselves for power. Some historians think the Vikings, originally from Scandinavia and traveling through the area in search of trade, were asked to bring order to the warring tribes. Others believe the Vikings invaded Slav territory. Whatever the case, the first Russian state, Kievan Rus, or simply Rus, was established in the ninth century in Kiev, in what is today Ukraine. It was ruled by a Viking grand prince.

The Rise of Muscovy and Russia

Rus remained isolated from the rest of Europe until the tenth century. In A.D. 988, Grand Prince Vladimir I became a Christian and made Christianity the official religion. Rus now observed the same religion as the rest of Christian Europe and enjoyed trade

IVAN THE TERRIBLE

Ivan the Terrible was the first ruler in Russia to use the title of tsar (czar). Not many people know that the first part of his reign was very productive for his country. It was only much later in life that he acquired his terrible reputation.
(*A Closer Look, page 55*)

THE COSSACKS

When Ivan the Terrible expanded his kingdom into Siberia, he enlisted the help of a remarkable group — the Cossacks.
(*A Closer Look, page 52*)

Left: In A.D. 988, Grand Prince Vladimir I converted to Christianity, choosing this religion from an array of other faiths that he had sent his advisors to experience firsthand. This painting shows the baptism of Vladimir.

with other European countries. But this golden period came to an abrupt end in the early thirteenth century when Genghis Khan led a powerful Mongolian invasion from the East. From 1240 until the fifteenth century, the Mongols ruled Rus. Although they destroyed Kiev, they were finally driven out of the country by grand princes based in Moscow.

The new empire became known in Western Europe as Muscovy, although its name remained Rus within the empire. Ivan the Terrible was the first to use the title of tsar. A long line of rulers gradually expanded the kingdom. During the reign of Peter the Great, from 1696 to 1725, Muscovy became the Empire of All Russias, or simply Russia, a change that reflected Peter's commitment to modernization. Unfortunately, weak rulers and rural poverty plagued Russia after Peter's death. Hatred for the tsars worsened with the Napoleonic Wars. Napoleon, self-crowned emperor of France, had conquered a large part of Europe by 1812. He tried to expand into Russia. Eventually, aided by a bitter winter, Russian troops chased a starving French army back to Paris. There, the Russians saw how backward Russia was, compared to the rest of Europe. They turned against their rulers, and the political situation was ripe for revolution.

Above: **Under serfdom — a system where landless peasants were forced to work for landowners — the nobility and landowners increasingly abused the peasants, or serfs.**

TOO LITTLE, TOO LATE

Throughout the nineteenth century, peasant revolts broke out all over the country with increasing frequency. The tsars suppressed the revolts violently, making themselves even more unpopular. Serfdom was abolished in 1861, but rural conditions remained so terrible that by the end of the nineteenth century, the whole fabric of Russian society was beginning to tear.

Revolution!

The year 1917 marked the beginning of an era that would become infamous in Russian and world history. In February, rebels forced Tsar Nicholas II to give up his throne. The rebels set up a parliament, but internal power struggles between different factions paralyzed the provisional government. In October, a minority party, the Bolsheviks, arrested the leaders of the provisional government. All power was now in the hands of one man, the leader of the Bolsheviks. His name was Vladimir Lenin.

Lenin instituted a form of government called communism. Conceived by German political philosopher Karl Marx, the theory of communism states that all people are equal. However, in its attempt to attain this and other communist ideals, Lenin's government restricted freedom of expression and religion in the U.S.S.R. When Lenin died in 1924, Josef Stalin succeeded him. Twenty million people died during Stalin's rigid, communist rule, many in concentration camps for forced labor. Russia suffered some of the worst setbacks in its entire history.

Above: **The October Revolution Parade in Moscow's Red Square in 1990. Until the U.S.S.R. collapsed in 1991, many parades and celebrations took place to commemorate the communists' rise to power in the U.S.S.R.**

COMMUNISM

In the U.S.S.R., the Communist Party attempted to achieve an equal society by pooling resources and sharing profits. But the ideals of communism proved difficult to put into practice, and the results were disastrous.
(A Closer Look, page 50)

World War II and After

In 1941, the German forces of Adolf Hitler invaded the U.S.S.R. Unprepared for war, Stalin's regime managed to defeat Germany only through the great sacrifices of the Russian people. Twenty-seven million Soviet people lost their lives during the war, which destroyed whole towns and villages. The Russians finally drove the Germans back and captured Berlin in 1945.

Severe political restrictions persisted long after World War II. It was only in 1987, after Mikhail Gorbachev rose to power, that things changed. He began to implement *perestroika* (pe-res-STROY-ka) and *glasnost* (GLAHS-nohst). Perestroika, or "restructuring," was a plan for economic reform. Glasnost, or "openness," was designed to give the Soviets greater freedom of expression and open up the U.S.S.R. to the rest of the world. Unfortunately, there was strong disagreement over how quickly these reforms should take place. On December 31, 1991, the U.S.S.R. was formally dissolved. The Russian Federation and eleven other former Soviet republics formed the Commonwealth of Independent States (CIS). Today, despite severe problems, Russia is moving toward a new future.

Above: **After the toppling of the communist regime, statues of former communist leaders, especially those of Lenin and Stalin, were often vandalized with graffiti or paint, removed from public places, and dumped.**

Left: **Despite the present government's commitment to democracy, a communist legacy remains. Occasional anti-reform demonstrations, such as this one, still occur. Behind the prominent banner depicting Lenin, the hammer-and-sickle motif on the flag of the former Soviet Union is partly visible.**

Peter the Great (1672–1725)

Peter the Great was a great man in many ways, including his height. He was 6 feet 8 inches (2 m) tall! By realizing his childhood dream of building a navy, he made Russia a world power. The first tsar to travel to Western Europe, he embarked on a Great Embassy that included visits to Great Britain, the United Provinces (now the Netherlands), and Prussia (now Germany). He took with him a company of about two hundred and fifty people, including court musicians. In Western Europe, Peter the Great studied shipbuilding and observed Western fashions. On returning, he implemented far-reaching reforms. By the time of his death, Russia had become the most powerful nation in Northern Europe.

Peter the Great

Catherine the Great (1729–1796)

Originally a German princess, Catherine the Great married Tsar Peter III, the grand-nephew of Peter the Great. Peter III ruled less than a year. When a revolt forced him to abdicate the throne, Catherine assumed power and further expanded Russia, conquering the northern coast of the Black Sea and a large part of Poland. Despite great territorial gains, there was trouble within Russia. Treated like slaves by their landowners, the serfs began to rebel against the tsarist regime. Various revolts shook the throne during and after Catherine's reign. She has also become famous for the dozen or so love affairs she conducted over a period of thirty years!

Opposite: **Catherine the Great reigned during a time of architectural and artistic flowering in Russia.**

Boris Yeltsin (1931–)

Yeltsin was born in Sverdlovsk (now Yekaterinburg) in the Ural Mountains. He worked in the construction industry before joining the Communist Party in 1961. In 1991, he became the first popularly elected Russian leader in history. Earlier that year, when hardline communists staged a coup against then Soviet leader Mikhail Gorbachev, Yeltsin stood on a tank in front of the Russian Parliament Building and defied the communists. After the coup failed, Yeltsin emerged as Russia's most influential politician. Committed to privatization and reform, he is a firm ruler, having managed to keep Russia in one piece despite his own health problems.

Boris Yeltsin

Government and the Economy

Toward a New Constitution

To understand how Russia is governed today, it is necessary to take a brief look at how it was ruled in the early twentieth century. After 1917 and the fall of Tsar Nicholas II, there was only one political party, the Communist Party of the Soviet Union. The so-called parliament agreed with everything the party dictated.

Rumblings of change began under Mikhail Gorbachev's leadership. Limited freedom of expression gave way to greater reforms. When Boris Yeltsin came to power at the end of 1991, he introduced many changes to the system of government. In 1993, Russia adopted a new constitution, based on the French model, which gives the president far-reaching powers. The president may veto and even dissolve the legislature when necessary. The president also appoints the prime minister, cabinet ministers, and court judges of the country.

Below: **Happy voters at a polling station in Moscow in March 1990. Democratic elections are a relatively recent and very welcome feature of political life in Russia.**

Parliament

The Russian parliament is called the Federal Assembly. It is made up of a Federation Council (the upper house) and the State Duma (the lower house). The Federation Council has 178 members who represent all the regions and republics that make up the Russian Federation. The State Duma has 450 seats. Its members are elected by proportional representation on a party basis, each member representing his or her own area or constituency.

The style of elections has changed since Soviet days. While there was hardly any campaigning in the past, election campaigns now resemble those in the United States, with rock bands playing in the squares and flags billowing in the streets and from buildings. Under communism, there had been only one party. Today, many parties exist, ranging from the conservative to the radical, and from the earnest to the eccentric.

The current head of state is President Boris Yeltsin, and the prime minister is Yevgeny Primakov. The main issues facing Russia's leaders today are economic revival and growth and the fight for political stability.

Above: **A meeting of the State Duma in 1996. The Duma has the right to express a no-confidence vote in the government, but may itself be disbanded by the president under certain special circumstances.**

Untold Natural Riches

Russia has a wealth of natural resources. It has the largest coal, oil, and natural gas reserves among the former Soviet republics. These abundant raw materials supported the economic achievements of the U.S.S.R. until the 1950s. In recent years, however, extracting these resources without serious financial investment has become increasingly difficult. For example, only a relatively small portion of Russia's huge oil reserves reaches the market. Old equipment tends to break down, making oil extraction very inefficient. In addition, leaky pipelines waste oil and cause serious environmental damage.

Russia experiences similar problems with the minerals it has in abundance — iron, nickel, lead, zinc, aluminum, and tin. Russia also has more valuable metals, such as tungsten, uranium, and gold. Unfortunately, many of these minerals are located in Siberia, where the harsh climate discourages mining activity. Foreign investment and expertise are beginning to help develop and open up the country, but it will be some time before these problems are solved.

Above: **Russia's abundant forests fuel a thriving wood and paper industry. Unfortunately, logging activities are also destroying the natural habitat of some species of wildlife.**

VALENTINA TERESHKOVA AND THE SPACE PROGRAM

In 1963, cosmonaut Valentina Tereshkova became the first woman in space. Some of the greatest achievements of the U.S.S.R. and Russia are in space exploration and research.
(A Closer Look, page 68)

Growing Industry and Trade

Russia's mineral riches support an advanced chemical industry as well as heavy engineering — the production of turbines, trains, cars, trucks, and airplanes. Many of these products are exported to developing countries worldwide. The energy to run these industries comes from coal-burning power stations. Because of the harshness of the climate, only about one-seventh of the land is suitable for growing crops. In Russia, fortunately, this is still a very large area! Grain is the most important crop. Russia now produces enough wheat, barley, rye, and oats to export a portion to other countries.

For decades, the average Russian lacked many of the conveniences of life that people elsewhere may take for granted — cars, a variety of food products, electrical goods, computers, and luxury goods. Russia did not have the money to import these goods or the infrastructure to manufacture them. Although these items are now pouring into Russia, the problem of distribution — or getting the goods to the places where they are needed — remains. Sometimes, factories lie idle because some crucial part has not been delivered.

CHERNOBYL

One of the worst disasters ever to hit the U.S.S.R. occurred in the early hours of April 16, 1986. Today, years after the explosion of a nuclear reactor at Chernobyl, the effects of the tragic accident are still being felt.
(A Closer Look, page 48)

Below: **Japanese cars being unloaded from a ship. Goods from all over the world arrive at Russia's ports each day.**

People and Lifestyle

Who Are the Russians?

About 85 percent of the people who live in Russia are described as Russians — people who belong to a group known as the East Slavs. This group includes the Ukrainians to the south of Russia and the Belarusians to the west. Ethnic Russians make up a majority of the population, but Russia consists of a diversity of peoples. There are twenty-one autonomous, or self-governing, minority republics in the Russian Federation. Because of this diversity, it is difficult to generalize about the appearance of Russians. Many foreigners have in mind the stereotype of a stocky, stern, and unsmiling people. Nothing could be further from the truth! There has been so much intermarriage between the ethnic groups over the centuries that many different traits are visible among them — Russians may be blond, dark-, or red-haired. They are a friendly and fun-loving people, often displaying a generosity that may surprise the Western visitor. Among more traditional Russians, there is still an element of suspicion regarding foreigners, but even this is vanishing rapidly as Russia opens its doors to the rest of the world.

MINORITY GROUPS

Fifteen percent of the population in Russia consists of more than seventy different ethnic groups. Only a few minorities — the Ukrainians, Chuvash, Bashkir, Belarusians, Mordvins, and Tatars — have more than a million members each.

(A Closer Look, page 60)

Left: Young women enjoying a walk in a park in Astrakhan.

Ethnic Unrest: Chechnya

Ethnic differences became more acute after the break-up of the Soviet Union. Some minority groups and autonomous regions have been fighting for greater recognition within Russia. Others want complete independence from the Russian Federation.

In 1994, the Russian government launched a war in Chechnya after the Chechen president, Dzhokhar Dudayev, rebelled against central rule. The action of the Russian government drew criticism from most of the other minority republics. Many of these republics, including Chechnya, are predominantly Muslim. They feel that their religion and identity are distinctly non-Russian. These ethnic issues have not yet been fully resolved.

THE REINDEER HERDERS OF THE NORTH

People do live in northern Russia despite the often severe cold. These reindeer herders belong to several different ethnic groups.
(A Closer Look, page 64)

Town and Countryside

Apart from ethnic divisions, perhaps the greatest difference among Russians is between urban and rural lifestyles. The large cities are prosperous and modernized, but life in the countryside is usually very different. In many ways, people in the countryside have lived the same way for centuries — in *izba* (IZ-ba), simple wooden houses. Although supplied with electricity, many of these houses do not have running water. People still use wells and carry buckets of water on a yoke, which is a wooden bar balanced over the shoulders.

Above: The famous GUM department store in Moscow was designed by A. N. Pomerantsev in the late nineteenth century. The store is usually crowded with shoppers and tourists browsing through a range of goods. Life in the countryside does not boast such luxury.

Family Life

About three-fourths of Russia's population is classified as urban. The biggest cities, Moscow and St. Petersburg, are far more densely populated than any of the other major cities in Russia. In urban areas, most people live in apartment buildings. They enjoy family pastimes, such as going to the movies, watching television, and playing games.

Family life in Russia often revolves around children, as it does in other parts of the world. Perhaps because older generations endured so much hardship in war and under the communist regime, children are especially treasured as the hope of the future. In the larger cities, families often enjoy day trips to amusement parks and puppet theaters for the children's sake. Outside almost every apartment building is a playground, often with an army of *babushki* (ba-BOOSH-kee) — grandmothers — sitting protectively around the toddlers! At home, many parents take the education of their children very seriously. They help them with homework or pay for private instruction in foreign languages and computer skills.

"NEW RUSSIANS"

A new class of Russians rose with capitalism. Much wealthier than the average Russian, these New Russians, as they are called, enjoy a luxurious lifestyle at home and abroad.
(*A Closer Look, page 62*)

Below: **Most Russians are friendly and get to know their neighbors well, stopping to exchange greetings and news when they meet.**

The Impact of Capitalism

The change from communism to capitalism has had a significant impact on family life in Russia. The communist government ensured that everyone had housing and employment, even if the standards of both were not always high. Capitalism provided better opportunities to make money, so many people began to work harder in order to improve their lives. Sometimes this hard work brought greater luxury. In other cases, however, family life at home suffered because many parents held more than one job to support their families.

While many families are better off under capitalism, extreme poverty has also emerged, especially among those too old to work. Overcrowding is another major problem in most Russian cities. Because apartments are either unavailable or too expensive for young couples, extended families of three generations sometimes live together in one apartment. Finally, homelessness is a problem, particularly for some of the very old or young. People too old to work are sometimes abandoned by their families. *Besprisorniki* (bes-pree-ZORN-ikee), the neglected children of broken homes, sometimes roam the streets.

Above: **A family celebration at Christmas. Today, many Russians lead busy lives at work, but getting together with friends and family is still important to them — perhaps reason enough to bring out the champagne!**

Going to School

Along with every other aspect of Russian life, the education system has recently undergone many fundamental changes. Since the fall of the Communist Party, compulsory political subjects, such as the theory and practice of communism and the story of Lenin's life, have been removed from the curriculum. In the past, the Communist Party strictly restricted information and controlled newspapers and all forms of public broadcasting. Today, the Russian media plays an important part in making information available to students and schools.

Preschool activities are well developed in Russia. A high percentage of children go to a day care or kindergarten. Free compulsory education begins at the age of seven. Students must attend school for at least eight years. In fact, about two-thirds of Russian children study for up to ten years. The system is thorough and tends to be somewhat stricter than in many countries in the West. Most children learn at least one foreign language; at the moment, the most popular one is English.

Above: **A day school in Russia. Children learn not only academic subjects, but also music and dance.**

Higher Education

Russia's oldest university was founded in 1755. Some fields of research suffered setbacks during the rule of the Communist Party, but Russia now produces many world-class scholars, especially in scientific research and development. Russian university professors of Russian literature and linguistics are also renowned worldwide in their fields. The best and most prestigious universities today include the Novosibirsk State University, the Moscow M. V. Lomonosov State University, and the St. Petersburg State University.

About 15 percent of the population has a higher education. Entry into a university depends on examination scores, a difficult and competitive process. An undergraduate degree in Russia normally takes five years. Here, again, the standards are very high. Many students experience great financial problems because scholarships and financial aid packages are rare.

Below: "I can't remember anything!" Examinations are an important yet stressful part of university entrance requirements in Russia.

The Russian Orthodox Church

Russian Orthodox Christianity is the national religion of Russia. Grand Prince Vladimir I made Christianity the state religion in the tenth century. In 1054, when the religion was split into the Orthodox and Catholic denominations, Russia adopted the Orthodox branch of the faith. There are also other Christian denominations in Russia, such as Baptist, Lutheran, and Catholic groups, but Russian Orthodox Christianity has been the dominant religion for nearly a thousand years.

Russian Orthodox beliefs are based on the Bible and emphasize faith and piety. Within the ornate churches, people light candles and burn incense as they pray. Opposite the west door of most churches, there is a panel of paintings that reaches the ceiling and separates the altar from the main body of the church. These paintings are called icons — holy images or objects traditionally used in worship or taken into battle for good fortune. Despite similarities with Roman Catholicism, the Russian Orthodox Church is led by the Patriarch of All Russia and does not recognize the pope.

Below: **A funeral procession. Russian Orthodox priests bear a coffin to the monastery of Tobolsk.**

Islam, Judaism, and Buddhism

After the years of intense persecution in the 1930s and 1940s and the restrictions of the Communist Party, true religious freedom has only recently become a reality.

Muslims form the second largest religious group in Russia. Their religion, Islam, has the greatest following among the Tatars, the Bashkirs, and some peoples in the northern Caucasus. Mosques are being built all over Russia as the religion enjoys renewed popularity.

During Stalin's rule and the German occupation, Russian Jews were persecuted. Since the late 1980s, increasing emigration to North America, Israel, and other parts of the world has decreased the Jewish population in Russia.

Today, relatively few ethnic Jews in the country still practice their faith. Most large towns in Russia have at least one synagogue, and Moscow has a rabbinical academy.

The majority of Buddhists in Russia live in the small republics of Buryatia (near Lake Baykal), Kalmykia (near the Caspian Sea), and Tuva (on the Mongolian border). Most of them speak Mongolian languages.

Above: **Crowds gather outside a Buddhist temple in Buryatia. Buddhism has a strong following in some minority republics.**

27

Language and Literature

The Cyrillic Alphabet

Russian is an East-Slavic language, closely related to Ukrainian and Belarusian. The most striking aspect of the Russian language is its unique alphabet. The Cyrillic alphabet is named after Cyril, who, with his brother Methodius, supposedly invented the alphabet for the Slav peoples in the ninth century. Cyril and Methodius, both monks, were later made saints in recognition of

Below: **A street sign in Moscow in the Cyrillic alphabet.**

their achievement. Loosely based on the Greek alphabet, the Cyrillic alphabet has thirty-three letters and is a phonetic alphabet. This means that by learning the letters and their sounds, one can pronounce almost any Russian word without difficulty.

Greetings!

Every Russian has three names: a given name; a patronymic name (a name derived from their father's first name); and a last name. For example, *Raisa Maksimovna Gorbacheva* would refer to Raisa, daughter of Maxim, Gorbachev. *Anton Pavlovich Chekhov* is Anton, son of Pavel, Chekhov. When greeting a Russian, it is polite to use the first two names. There are other rules and customs in greeting Russians. For instance, the first name of a close friend may be shortened — *Alexander* becomes *Sasha*.

Literature

Early Russian writings are important historical documents. For example, the *Tale of Bygone Years* is a chronicle, or historical narrative, of important events in the eleventh century. Despite a long tradition of writing, Russia's greatest contribution to world literature is probably its astonishing nineteenth-century output. Alexander Pushkin (1799–1837), Nikolai Gogol (1809–1852), Ivan Turgenev (1818–1883), Fyodor Dostoevsky (1821–1881), and Leo

LITERARY GREATS

Alexander Pushkin and Leo Tolstoy are considered two of Russia's most talented writers. Their works show the realities of Russian life in the nineteenth century, as well as the creative imagination of Russian literary greats.
(A Closer Look, page 59)

Tolstoy (1828–1910) are considered among the world's greatest poets and writers. The mid-nineteenth century saw the rise of realism, a movement characterized by a detailed description of real life. While Dostoevsky evoked the frustration of the powerless Russian citizen, Turgenev took on social issues, such as serfdom, in his writing.

More recently, Russia has also produced famous literary figures, such as the playwright and short story writer Anton Chekhov (1860–1904) and the writer Boris Pasternak (1890–1960). Nobel Prize winners include Mikhail Sholokhov (1905–1984), Joseph Brodsky (1940–1996), and Alexander Solzhenitsyn (1918–).

Above: A bookseller in St. Petersburg. Russians are avid readers and appreciate literature.

Arts

Folk Arts and Crafts

Russian folk art has a long and interesting history. In the past, before roads and railways opened up most of the vast country, traveling through unexplored and harsh terrain was difficult. In remote villages, people turned to arts and crafts to amuse themselves during the long, cold winter nights.

One popular pastime was spinning. Russian women spun thread from wool, using equipment — the distaff and spinning wheel — that was often beautifully decorated. Ornate lacquer boxes first appeared in the late eighteenth century. Brightly and elaborately hand-painted, these boxes depict scenes from Russian folk tales. Tourists are not the only ones who find Russian painted bowls, nesting dolls, and lacquered boxes irresistible — almost every Russian household has a collection of them. *Matriyoshki* (ma-tree-OSH-kee) dolls are among the most charming of crafted items. Within the largest doll nestles a similar, smaller one, and

Below: **Matriyoshki dolls are probably the most famous items of Russian folk art. They are made out of birch wood and beautifully hand-painted.**

within that, another, and so on, right down to the tiniest doll. Today, crafts are sold at the Istoki Gallery in Moscow. These range from pottery, ceramics, and embroidery, to ragdolls and puppets. Moscow's Museum of Applied Folk Art also showcases traditional arts and crafts.

Above: **A traditional Russian music group performs in Poland. Groups like this often travel within Russia as well as across Europe.**

Traditional and Classical Music

The Russian national instruments include the *balalaika* (bal-al-AI-ka), psaltery, reed-pipe, and accordion. The balalaika is a triangular stringed instrument played by plucking or strumming. The psaltery is a medieval stringed instrument.

Russia, like Austria and Italy, has produced many outstanding classical composers and musicians. Probably the most famous is Peter Tchaikovsky (1840–1893), who composed the *Nutcracker Suite* and *Swan Lake.* Other talented composers include Nicolai Rimsky–Korsakov (1844–1908), Sergei Rachmaninoff (1873–1943), Sergei Prokofiev (1891–1953), and Igor Stravinsky (1882–1971). Stravinsky's ballet, *The Firebird,* brought him international fame. Many films today have soundtracks that borrow themes from the Russian composers.

CONTEMPORARY MUSIC

Some things, it seems, are universal — Western rock and pop music are popular with Russian youth today. Jazz, once discouraged, is now enjoying renewed interest and appreciation. And there is now even Russian rap music!

Ballet

Russia is home to two of the world's greatest ballet companies —
the Bolshoi and the Kirov (formerly Mariinsky). Russian ballet
had humble beginnings in the eighteenth century, but rose to
achieve worldwide acclaim. The late Galina Ulanova was among
the greatest dancers of classical ballet this century. Famous
dancers who defected (emigrated for political reasons) from the
U.S.S.R. include Rudolf Nureyev, Mikhail Baryshnikov, and
Natalia Makarova.

Above: **Ballet has
always been one of
Russia's successes.**

Painting

Early Russian painting was mainly of icons depicting religious
or political figures. These images often symbolized greater
concepts, such as holiness, courage, or freedom. In the nineteenth
century, great Russian realist painters Vasily Vereshchagin
(1842–1904) and Ilya Repin (1844–1930) emerged. However, many
Russian artists emigrated before the October Revolution. After
Lenin and the Bolsheviks gained power, Russian-born painters
Vasily Kandinsky (1866–1944) and Marc Chagall (1887–1985)
helped develop modern art movements in Western Europe.

Below: The Epic Heroes,
**by Viktor Vasnetsov
(1848–1926), depicts
fourteenth-century Rus
warriors who fought
against the Mongols.**

Architecture

Over the centuries, Russian architecture has been influenced by many different movements. The oldest structures still standing today include churches, fortresses, and monasteries. Russia's unique domed churches are surely among the most breathtaking buildings in the world. Many of them date back to Kievan Rus in the eleventh and twelfth centuries!

In the Middle Ages, Russian rulers had to defend their towns from enemy invasions. They ordered strong walls built around these towns. Architects also designed fortresses with tall towers for watchmen. Moscow's White City is an example of a sixteenth-century fortress.

In the countryside today, many people still build wooden houses in the traditional style, which has not changed much since the Middle Ages. While public buildings are still designed and constructed with traditional styles and building methods, new urban residential blocks now resemble those in Western European countries. High-rise apartment projects are being built at an astonishing pace. A wealthy class of "New Russians" is also building modern houses in new estates.

BUILDINGS AND SKYLINES

From the traditional domed churches to the regular geometric blocks of the 1930s and 1940s, Russian architecture has seen many phases. Today, these different buildings make Russian cities some of the most beautiful in the world.

(A Closer Look, page 46)

Leisure and Festivals

Favorite Pastimes . . .

What do Russians do in their free time? When in power, the Communist Party built recreational centers in the villages. These contained libraries, theaters, and activity halls. Today, leisure activities are less planned and more similar to those enjoyed all over the world. Families host dinner parties and relax in front of the television; young people go shopping, play games, or challenge one another in sports. To a great extent, Russian hobbies depend on personal interests. Many people are keen readers. Others enjoy craft projects or learn to play musical instruments. Outdoor activities, such as cycling and running, are also popular.

LET'S PICK MUSHROOMS!

Imagine strolling through the forest on a glorious autumn day. Russians enjoy just that when they indulge in a favorite outdoor activity, picking mushrooms.
(A Closer Look, page 56)

Left: **Winter does not deter the determined Russian fisherman!**

. . . With a Twist!

Although most Russian pastimes are familiar to us, some of them take an interesting twist. For example, winter swimming is a great favorite in Russia. Russians claim it is excellent for the skin and for circulation. Before their dip, people go into a *banya* (BAN-ya), or steam bath, to relax and enjoy the hot steam. Then, they go outside, dig a hole in the ice on a river or lake, and plunge into the cold water, wearing nothing more than swimsuits! Men often compete to see who can stay in the icy water longest.

Fishing is another passion — and not just in summer. It is not unusual for people to go out onto a frozen river in the middle of winter, drill a hole in the ice, and hope that a fish might take the bait. People sometimes wrap a huge plastic sheet around themselves, forming a "tent" to keep in the warmth as they wait for the fish to bite.

Another popular Russian hobby is chess. Almost everywhere, players can be seen with their heads bent in concentration over chess boards. Little wonder, then, that many of the best chess champions in the world are Russian!

Above: **People all over the world play chess, but perhaps none with the enthusiasm and dedication of Russians!**

WEEKEND AT A DACHA

Living space in the city is often cramped, and life, hectic. When Russians get tired of the city crowds, many retreat to charming houses in the countryside.
(*A Closer Look, page 70*)

Left: **Gymnast Alexei Voropayev, a candidate for the Russian Olympic team in 1996. The 1996 Olympic Games, held in Atlanta in the United States, marked the first time that Russia and the other former Soviet nations all fielded separate teams.**

Sporting Achievements

The U.S.S.R. took great political pride in sporting excellence. Soviet gymnasts; track-and-field athletes; ice hockey, volleyball, and basketball players all won numerous medals in international competitions. A sports champion could look forward to a life better than the average Russian could hope to attain. Today, sports are still regarded as important in Russia, and they are a vital part of extracurricular activities in schools. Any budding star can expect to receive as much help as the state can afford.

The U.S.S.R. is probably best remembered for its talented gymnasts, notably Olga Korbut, who charmed the world with her routines in the 1972 Olympics, winning three gold medals. In the 1992 Olympics, the last time the CIS and Georgia fielded a united team, Vitaly Shcherbo won a record six gold medals. The United Team also swept gold medals in several events, including long-distance walking, pole vault, hammer throw, shot put, women's

WINTER FUN

From snow sports to winter swimming, Russians show their creativity and love of the outdoors even in the harshest of climates.
(A Closer Look, page 72)

women's basketball, and canoeing. For many years, ice skating was also dominated by Russia. Irina Rodnina won ten pairs titles with two different partners — Alexei Ulanov and then, her husband, Alexander Zaytsev. In fact, Russian teams fill the Guinness Book of Records with their sports accomplishments. The greatest number of gold medals ever won by an individual is an astounding eighteen, by Soviet gymnast Larissa Latynina (1934–), in a remarkable career that spanned several local and international competitions! Other popular sports in Russia include soccer, skiing, and horse racing. The native Russian

Below: **A troika. It takes a lot of skill to manage a team of three spirited horses.**

version of horse racing is the *troika* (TROY-ka). A troika is a sleigh drawn by a team of three horses. This sport is the subject of many folk songs.

Pursuing Careers in the West

The Communist Party did not permit athletes to turn professional. Today, however, Russian sports stars are discovering that they can earn much more money outside of Russia. Many of them have signed contracts to join teams in Western Europe and North America. Some of Russia's top soccer players are now playing for Western European teams for very high salaries.

Left: Parents and children surround Father Frost and the Snow Maiden, two popular Christmas figures in Russia.

Religious Festivals

When the communists swept into power in 1917, all religious holidays were banned. Today, however, religion, along with its festive occasions, is enjoying a revival.

Russian Christians love Christmas and Easter as much as Christians in other countries. At Shrovetide, called Butter Week in Russia, people enjoy a huge feast, their last before the fasting period of Lent begins. Butter Week festivities illustrate the blending of Christian and pagan practices in Russian tradition. Although Lent has a Christian significance, during Shrovetide, people eat *bliny* (BLEE-nye) — round pancakes representing the pagan sun god, Yarilo. People also burn an effigy, a straw figure symbolizing winter, to bid the season good-bye.

Russian Muslims, like other Muslims around the world, observe the Prophet Muhammad's birthday and the celebrations marking the end of Ramadan, their month of fasting.

Ethnic Celebrations

The most popular ethnic festivals in Russia date back to pre-Christian times. Rooted in pagan celebrations of the end of winter and the rites of spring, the festivals of Sabantui (Sah-bant-OOEH), Navruz (Nahv-ROOZ), and Surkharban (Soor-kah-BAHN) all pay tribute to the start of a new agricultural year and the blossoming of spring flowers.

Sabantui is celebrated by the Tatars to mark the sowing of crops in the spring. Navruz is a Muslim festival celebrating the arrival of spring. It often takes on a vibrant air as people parade in the village streets, singing songs and carrying flowers. The Buryats celebrate Sukharban, their crop-sowing festival, with archery and wrestling competitions, as well as horse racing.

In certain parts of the countryside, festivals are accompanied by singing and chanting. People perform a *chastushka* (chahs-TOOSH-ka), a four-line verse set in rhythm to balalaika or accordion music. The verses often comment on local news, with two or more performers competing to compose the wittiest verses as the crowds cheer their favorite singers.

Below: **A Sabantui celebration in Tatarstan. Ethnic festivals are colorful and lively events.**

Food

Russian food is substantial — it has to be, to fortify people against the winter cold! Traditionally, Russian tsars impressed their guests with lavish dinners that were feasts for the eye, as well as for the stomach.

Soups are an important item on the Russian menu. *Borshch* (BORSH), a Ukrainian soup made from beets, is popular throughout Russia. *Solyanka* (sol-YAN-ka), a thick broth with meat and vegetables, is almost a meal on its own.

Appetizers, called *zakuski* (ZAK-oos-kee), consist of various dishes, such as caviar (the salted roe of the sturgeon, a large fish), bliny, eel or salmon, and mushrooms in cream. Salted herring, salted or pickled mushrooms, and salads are also popular choices

A Russian meal is accompanied by bread. Main courses consist of meat and vegetables. Some Russian dishes, such as beef Stroganoff and chicken Kiev, are so well-known worldwide that we sometimes forget their Russian origin. *Pelmeni* (PEL-me-nee) is Siberian ravioli; *shashlyk* (shash-LIK) are lamb kebabs served with

Below: **Pelmeni is served with other dishes, such as chicken and mushrooms.**

a hot, red sauce. Pork is a very popular meat in Russia. It is often served with garlic sauce and cheese. *Smetana* (SMET-ana), sour cream, is added to almost everything, especially soups.

Desserts often consist of fruit, but Russian ice cream is also first-class! The national drink is vodka, a very strong, clear liquor made out of wheat or rye. Russian champagne is also excellent. Tea is served without milk, and sometimes accompanied with homemade jam. Traditional Russian tea has a strong aroma and is made in large tea urns called *samovary* (SAM-o-VA-ree). When invited to an evening meal, it is very impolite even to hint at leaving before tea is served!

An Expanding Menu

The Russian diet has been changing since imported foods became more readily available in the shops. Cooking in the home has become much more inventive than in the past, and the number of restaurants is also increasing. Today, cuisine from almost every nationality is represented in the city restaurants, catering to ever more adventurous taste buds!

Above: **A fruit seller tempts passersby with his trays of fresh apples and pears. A serving of fruit often rounds off a typical Russian meal.**

A CLOSER LOOK AT RUSSIA

Russian civilization extends over a thousand years. From amazing churches and skylines to the beautiful Siberian tiger and burly brown bear, Russia boasts unique features, both manmade and natural, that deserve a closer look.

Modern Russia has emerged from a complicated and colorful past. While some of Russia's rulers brought peace and prosperity, many also subjected the country to wars and great hardship, destroying the achievements of previous generations. The work of

literary giants such as Alexander Pushkin and Leo Tolstoy flourished, but later communist rule stifled freedom of expression in the U.S.S.R. The country had an excellent space program responsible for sending the first woman, Valentina Tereshkova, into space — but also had a nuclear disaster of tragic proportions at Chernobyl.

The disintegration of the U.S.S.R. had far-reaching effects on the Russian people. Encouraged by the independence of former Soviet republics, many of Russia's minority republics continue to preserve and assert their ethnic identity. The introduction of capitalism has also seen the steady rise of a new class of wealthy Russians who are exploiting a budding market economy.

Above: **In Kamchatka, children celebrate the end of winter in vibrant costumes.**

Opposite: **Communist demonstrators in Mayakovsky Square in Moscow. Such groups are violently opposed to democratic reforms in Russia.**

The Brown Bear

Russia is often identified with the large brown bear. In fact, the bear was the mascot chosen for the 1980 Olympic Games held in Moscow. The animal is regarded as a brave, noble creature and is admired for its great strength.

Bear cubs are usually born in winter. They grow rapidly and venture out into the world by late spring, under the watchful eye of their mother. The father plays no part in their upbringing. Bear cubs spend a great deal of time playing, swimming in rivers, and

Left: **Brown bears have been part of traveling animal shows in Russia for hundreds of years.**

tumbling around with other cubs. Mother bears defend their young fiercely from predators and hunters, but, as cubs grow older, they learn to forage for food and survive independently. Brown bears love honey, and their long claws enable them to rip open beehives to reach the honeycombs. Their thick, furry coats protect them from bee stings. Bears also thrive on a diet of fish, nuts, berries, and other fruit. In the autumn, they begin to fatten up for the long winter months ahead. After feeding generously, they head for their winter lair — a cave or a thicket in which to spend the coldest months. The Russian bears do not hibernate in the strict sense of the word; they do go to sleep, but wake up from time to time. Only when spring comes again do they resume a more active life.

Above: **The cuddly appearance of the brown bear belies its ferocious nature when attacked. Possessing razor-sharp teeth and claws and weighing up to 560 pounds (255 kilograms), an adult bear may be as tall as 7 feet (2.1 m) when standing upright on its hind legs.**

A Dwindling Population

The population of brown bears in Russia is less than forty thousand. Their main enemy, unfortunately, is humankind. Despite being a protected species, bears are often hunted for sport and for their fur. Bear's paw is also considered a food delicacy in some parts of northeastern Russia.

Buildings and Skylines

Where Heaven Meets Earth

Who could fail to marvel at Russia's great domed churches, especially St. Basil's on Red Square in Moscow? The oldest stone churches were built during the eleventh and twelfth centuries. Gradually, the structure of churches became more and more uniform, and a distinctly Russian church developed.

The traditional form of a Russian church is usually a cube topped by a dome. This structure symbolizes Earth, with heaven above it. The ceiling of each cube is supported by four massive pillars. The domes are usually colorful and elaborately designed. The number of domes in each church may vary. Each number has a special significance — one represents Jesus Christ; three, the Trinity; and five, Jesus and four apostles. Although white limestone is the most common building material, some of the oldest churches are architectural wonders built entirely out of wood, with no other tools except the axe. Not a single nail enters

Below, left and *right:* **These churches show variations in the style of Russian Orthodox churches. Domes and facades range from the simple to the ornate.**

Left: **The imposing facade of the Lenin Memorial in Lenin Square in Khabarovsk.**

these structures! Instead, the beams are firmly held in place by wooden pegs or by horizontally interlocking corners. Many of these old wooden churches have withstood the severe climate and are still in good condition today.

A Variety of Architectural Styles

When Peter the Great moved the Russian capital from Moscow to St. Petersburg in the early eighteenth century, he invited architects from Italy and Germany to transform St. Petersburg in the image of Western Europe. Later, Catherine the Great hired many French architects to design buildings in the Baroque style. The period of her rule also produced two outstanding Russian architects trained abroad — Vasily Bazhenov (1737–1799) and Matvei Kazakov (1738–1812). The early twentieth century saw a revival of the neoclassical style; for example, large, classical columns support the Lenin Library in Moscow. In the Stalinist era, huge structures were built to impress — to make the onlooker feel dwarfed by giant, forbidding concrete blocks. Today, modern housing in Russia closely resembles apartment buildings in Western Europe and North America.

Chernobyl

At 1:23 a.m. on April 16, 1986, the fire alarms at a nuclear power station about 65 miles (105 km) north of Kiev, Ukraine, started ringing. No one imagined the events of that day would bring Chernobyl worldwide infamy.

At first, fearing blame, no one responsible for the power plant reported what had happened. The U.S.S.R., still in the era of closed doors, denied that anything disastrous had taken place. It was a U.S. satellite that captured the raging fire within the plant. The top of the reactor had been blown off, allowing radioactive dust and gases to escape! The radiation spread throughout Russia and toward Western Europe, and was first detected by the Swedes. When rain fell, it contaminated the plants that fed cattle and sheep, and affected the reindeer in the north. The results of the disaster were more tragic than anyone could have predicted — 31 people died as an immediate result of the accident, another 300 were hospitalized, and 135,000 evacuated from their homes in the area.

Below: **Within two weeks of the explosion at Chernobyl, many nearby Russian towns, such as this one, stood evacuated and empty.**

In all, about 8 tons (7.3 metric tons) of radioactive dust and gases were released into the atmosphere. Although the accident happened in the Ukraine, inhabitants of Russian towns within a wide radius of the power plant were all affected by the radiation. The invisible pollutants harmed millions of unsuspecting victims directly and indirectly. Besides the immediate victims of radiation sickness, there is the risk of birth defects in the future. Mutant species of plants have been found. As far away as England, whole flocks of sheep in the mountains were infected. Many Russian children are now suffering from leukemia, a cancer of the blood that can be caused by exposure to high levels of radiation. Chernobyl's final death toll, therefore, remains to be seen.

Russian authorities covered the damaged reactor with reinforced concrete, creating a shield they call a "sarcophagus" — a word originally used to describe an ancient Egyptian coffin or tomb. Chernobyl's aptly named sarcophagus is a memorial to the dead and a grim reminder of the danger of nuclear power. The sarcophagus will have to remain in place for hundreds of years before radiation levels finally fall within a safe range.

Above: **Aerial view of the Chernobyl nuclear reactor about a year after the accident. The sarcophagus is the black, concrete structure built around the reactor.**

Communism

Leninism

Communism began as an academic theory of German philosopher Karl Marx (1818–1883). Marx envisioned a fair and just government and social system, in which the people would rule themselves and share whatever they produced. There would be no classes or hierarchies; everyone would be equal and equally looked after.

When Lenin seized power after the October Revolution of 1917, he adapted these ideas and tried to put them into practice. Under Lenin, the Russian states became the U.S.S.R. (Union of Soviet Socialist Republics). The capital reverted to Moscow, and Tsar Nicholas and his family were murdered. To create a complete break with the past, even private property was abolished. Lenin's Communist Party set up collective farms to accumulate the

Left: **A salute to communism. A poster of Lenin hangs from a building in Yaroslavl during the Soviet era. Whether Lenin's system of government can properly be called communism is doubtful, since Marx's ideals had never before been implemented. Lenin imposed his own visions on Marx's theory, and some historians call Lenin's version "Leninism."**

nation's agricultural produce and redistribute it equally across the country. Unfortunately, the Party imposed such a strict quota on each farm that the workers suffered greatly while trying to meet those demands. Many people objected to these policies, and the civil war continued. Lenin then set up a police force, the *Cheka* (CHEK-a), to eliminate his enemies by any means possible.

Above: **In 1929, under the collectivization scheme, all land became state-owned. Harvesters on collective farms often gathered to listen to propaganda about communist values.**

Stalinism and Beyond

Lenin's successor, Josef Stalin, continued a tyrannical rule. In general, he used propaganda — promoting and publicizing himself through the media — so successfully that many ordinary people loved him. He ruled over the remaining population by fear. His policy was to make people believe there was a spy around every corner. Even his closest "friends" were not safe from being sentenced to the firing squad or exiled to Siberia.

This oppressive atmosphere survived long past Stalin's death. Only in the last thirty years or so have mounting pressures from the West, government reforms, and groups within Russia succeeded in toppling the Communist Party. Even so, anti-democracy lobbies still exist in Russia today.

The Cossacks

When Ivan the Terrible opened up Siberia in the sixteenth century, he had the help of a rugged and dedicated group — the Cossacks. Today, they are often better remembered for their dances than for their role in Russian history. Who are these remarkable people?

The Cossacks are not a nationality but rather a borderland people made up of Russians, Poles, Lithuanians, and Ukrainians. For various reasons, they left their own countries to live a free life on the Russian borders, over which no one had effective political control. Many were serfs who had escaped from their landlords. Some were exiles, others adventurers.

They moved to the north of the Caucasus Mountains and settled as various agricultural–military groups, such as the Don Cossacks, the Zaporozhian Cossacks, and the Kuban Cossacks. Great fighters and horsemen, they would serve anyone who offered them the best deal — not necessarily the tsar! The first famous Cossack was Yermak. Along with about sixteen hundred Cossacks, he crossed the Ural Mountains under the orders of a

Below: The Cossacks Drafting a Letter to the Turkish Sultan, a **painting by Ilya Repin.**

rich merchant named Stroganoff. In 1582, the Cossack army entered Siberia and, although outnumbered, defeated the local leaders. Ivan the Terrible was only too pleased to accept the new lands offered to him by Stroganoff and began the eastern expansion of the Russian empire.

Another well-known Cossack leader was Stenka Razin, a Don Cossack. Proclaiming freedom for all peasants, he massacred many nobles around the Volga region in 1670. Eventually, he mustered a following of twenty thousand men. He was defeated on his way to Moscow and executed in 1671. The Cossack Pugachev went even further than Razin. Pugachev pretended to be Tsar Peter III, the husband of Catherine the Great. In 1773, he led a revolt against Catherine, promising freedom from serfdom, taxation, and military service — issues that have plagued Russian leaders throughout history. Pugachev was defeated in 1774 and cruelly executed. As seen in their colorful history, the Cossacks are more than skillful horsemen. They opened up Siberia and fought for the rights of the underprivileged, as well as for their own interests.

Above: **Cossacks in traditional dress. In 1917, the Cossacks were banned from the country by the communist regime for being allies with government enemies. Today, the Cossack people and their traditions are thriving.**

Ivan the Terrible

Ivan IV ruled Russia (then called Muscovy) from 1533 to 1584. His Russian nickname, *grozny* (GROHZ-nye), properly means "awe-inspiring," rather than "terrible." Contrary to the common belief, Ivan's reign was not wholly destructive. His reputation for cruelty was acquired only in the last part of his long rule.

Ivan the Terrible was only three when his father died in 1533. Until he was able to assert his own power, the nobles in his court struggled bitterly among themselves, treating the young ruler badly. In 1547, Ivan proclaimed himself tsar of Russia. "Tsar" means "emperor." Ivan wanted to distinguish his reign from that of the grand princes of the now fallen Kievan Rus. He fought and defeated the invading Tatars, or Mongols, securing for Muscovy the whole of the Volga as far as the Caspian Sea. He then turned west and fought the Poles and Lithuanians, expanding his empire even farther and establishing trade with England. Therefore, the early part of Ivan's reign was extremely productive.

Things started to change in 1553, when Ivan fell dangerously ill. His followers and advisors would not accept his son Dmitri as the next tsar. In 1560, his wife, Anastasia Romanovna, died. A grief-stricken Ivan left Moscow. When the people begged him to come back, he set up an organization called the *Oprichniki* (ah-PREECH-ni-kee) — a kind of secret police of about six thousand, who wore black and rode black horses. The Oprichniki was ordered to destroy anybody who opposed Ivan. By this time, Ivan was apparently losing his mind. Legend has it that he blinded the architects of St. Basil's, so they would not build a cathedral more splendid. He killed his son Ivan in a fit of rage. He married another six times, but these marriages were unhappy. At one stage, he even expressed an interest in marrying Queen Elizabeth I of England!

Nevertheless, Muscovy progressed under Ivan's reign, learning from the West and gaining territory. With the help of the Cossacks, Ivan opened up Siberia. Despite his cruelty in suppressing his enemies, he continued to enjoy popular support within his kingdom. But Muscovy was only outwardly and tenuously held together by Ivan's rigid decrees. This superficial order gave way to power struggles when he died.

Above: **The high priest Philip rebuking Ivan the Terrible — to little avail.**

Opposite: **Ivan the Terrible wearing Monomakh's Cap. The oldest of the tsars' crowns, it probably dates back to the thirteenth or fourteenth century.**

Let's Pick Mushrooms!

Berry or apple picking is a common activity in the West in the summer or autumn — but what about mushrooms? In Russia, hundreds of people armed with wicker baskets venture into the forests on summer and autumn weekends to hunt down their favorite mushrooms! Moving into the forests, they head away from the main roads, where pollution is worst. They mark the trees at regular intervals, so as not to get lost. Certain varieties of mushrooms are poisonous, so an expert teaches the pickers which ones to leave alone.

Mushroom picking is also an opportunity to experience the beauty of the countryside and a chance to enjoy the company of friends and family. Mushroom pickers are usually prepared for a friendly competition to collect the most and choicest mushrooms. The whole family participates with enthusiasm. Children sometimes play a trick on their unsuspecting parents, padding the bottom of their basket with moss, then piling mushrooms on top, so the basket looks fuller than it really is!

Below: **Mushroom pickers take a break to inspect the contents of their baskets.**

There are over four hundred edible varieties of mushrooms in Russia. They come in all shapes, sizes, and colors, including red, yellow, brown, and white. The Russian favorite is the delicious penny bun (*Boletus edulis*). The lucky person who discovers a patch of these mushrooms instantly wins the picking competition hands down.

Mushrooms are a favorite food, and Russians have several ways of preparing them. Here is one recipe for the day's pickings. Make sure the mushrooms used are not poisonous.

Boil and mash some potatoes. Add chopped onion and an egg yolk to the mash. Roll the mash out into circles on a floured board. Boil some mushrooms, and fry them with chopped onion, garlic, salt, and pepper. Put a small ball of the mix into the center of each potato pastry circle. Fold the pastry over the mix, so the pieces look like crescents. Coat the pieces with egg-white, and dip them in bread crumbs. Then, fry them in oil or bake them in the oven at 350° F (180° C) until they are golden brown. This recipe yields a batch of delicious potato and mushroom pies.

Above: **Fresh mushrooms for sale in a market in Russia. Mushrooms may be eaten fresh, pickled, or dried. They may also be combined with other ingredients to produce a tasty dish.**

Literary Greats

Alexander Pushkin

Alexander Pushkin's background was unusual. His father was from an established noble family. His mother, according to family lore, was the granddaughter of a captured Abyssinian who became a high-ranking officer in Peter the Great's army.

In 1820, Pushkin was exiled from Moscow for writing anti-tsarist poems. Although he did not take part in the Decembrist Revolt of 1825 — in which army officers rebelled against Tsar Nicholas I — he sympathized with the rebels. Pushkin's punishment involved having the tsar himself as a personal censor. Pushkin could not publish anything without Nicholas's prior approval. This, however, did not stop Pushkin from mastering his art. He put his remarkable talents to writing poetry, short stories, and novels, excelling in all. Today, he is widely credited with the creation of the modern Russian literary language.

Six years after marrying the beautiful Natalia Goncharova, Pushkin became jealous of a man named D'Anthès. He challenged D'Anthès to a duel and wounded him, but Pushkin himself was fatally shot.

Above: **Alexander Pushkin is widely considered Russia's national poet.**

Opposite: **Leo Tolstoy, photographed in 1908.**

Leo Tolstoy

Leo Tolstoy was born into nobility in 1828. As a young man, he was a soldier in the Crimean War (1853–1856), a conflict between Russia and Britain, France, and Ottoman Turkey over Russian Orthodox subjects in Ottoman territories. Tolstoy also traveled in Western Europe. These experiences contributed to his natural sensitivity to social problems and to human nature in all its restless passion. In his later years, Tolstoy became increasingly concerned with the purpose and meaning of life. He nurtured a private desire to abandon material comforts for a wandering lifestyle. In 1910, he was found dead at a railway station, having left home suddenly and without explanation one night.

Tolstoy's novels display an astonishing sympathy for the circumstances and behavior of his characters. In *Anna Karenina*, he tells the tragic story of a beautiful, married woman whose love affair with a younger, dashingly handsome man destroys her marriage, and gradually her own life.

Minority Groups

Fifteen percent of Russia's population, or about twenty-three million people, belong to minority groups. Many of these groups live in autonomous republics in the Russian Federation. The largest group, the Turkic speakers, include the Bashkir, Chuvash, Tatars, and Tuvans. Many of these peoples became part of Russia as their lands were conquered throughout the centuries. For instance, the Bashkir are Muslims who came under Russian rule in the sixteenth century. The Chuvash are Orthodox Christians probably descended from the medieval Volga Bulgarians. Other minorities speak the Manchu-Tungus and Mongolian languages. Some Mongols, such as the Buryats and the Kalmyks, remained in Russia after their rulers were driven back from Russian territories by Ivan the Terrible. The once large Jewish population in Russia dwindled because of persecution in the early and mid-twentieth

Below: **Women in Tatarian clothes in Kazan, Tatarstan.**

Left: **A Chukchi girl in traditional dress. The Chukchi are a northern people who depend mainly on reindeer for a living.**

century, followed by increased emigration to Israel and other parts of the world in the 1980s and 1990s. Russia also has a tiny population of Gypsies. In the past, the Gypsies wandered throughout the country, visiting peasant markets and festivals and telling fortunes or trading horses for a living. Today, however, many have settled into permanent homes, and their wandering lifestyle is slowly vanishing.

National Costumes

Folk costumes embody the culture of the Russian and minority peoples. In the far north, traditional dress is adapted to the environment; fur coats play a vital part in keeping the Yakut warm. National costumes also reflect the wearers' beliefs. In the past, people wore embroidered garments for both decorative and superstitious reasons. They believed the embroidery on men's shirts and the ornaments on men's and women's clothing would ward off evil spirits. Today, few of these superstitions survive, but Russians remain proud of their national costumes and wear them during festivals and on special occasions.

"New Russians"

When the U.S.S.R. dissolved in 1991, big changes took place in everyday lifestyles. A strict, almost military regime, with very little room for initiative, gave way to a market economy. The result was a new social class — the so-called "New Russians."

Who is a New Russian? The main distinguishing characteristic is money — lots of it. Some New Russians have accumulated millions of rubles in recent years. Many of them are shrewd businesspeople who saw a gap in the market and filled it. Before 1991, many goods taken for granted in the West were unheard of in Russia. This created a golden opportunity for people to get rich quick when Russia opened its doors to foreign trade. Businesspeople imported and marketed new goods, such as the latest electronic equipment, Western fashion, jewelry, cars, and food items from around the world. These successful entrepreneurs soon became known as New Russians.

Below: **Wealthy Russians outside a new restaurant in Moscow, "Paradise Yard."**

Above: **New Russian houses in Samara. Many of these are substantially bigger than the houses of average Russians.**

Not all New Russian business activities are legal. For example, the Russian mafia makes money from protection rackets and organized crime. Western investment is helping the Russian government deal with these and other problems, such as smuggling and drug trafficking.

New Russians have a lifestyle very different from the average Russian. Their chauffeurs drive them around in the grandest and most expensive cars. They build huge houses near Moscow and St. Petersburg, wear expensive clothes, and spend their holidays in top resorts throughout the world. Many are now buying luxury properties in the south of France, London, and Switzerland. All over Moscow and St. Petersburg, luxury restaurants, clubs, and casinos are springing up to cater to this new class of Russians.

What do average Russians think about this new class? Many are not at all impressed. Envy may account for a lot of their dislike, because the New Russians are very, very rich compared to the average Russian, who earns less than U.S. $300 a month. But some Russians say they object more to the behavior than to the earnings of the New Russians and complain about their disregard for the less fortunate.

The Reindeer Herders of the North

Reindeer differ from other species of deer in that both sexes have antlers. Males frequently have majestic, branched antlers, which sometimes break off in fights with other males; those of the females are smaller. Reindeer have large hooves that spread out for good balance when they walk on snow or soggy ground. Their herds vary in size in the wild, from about eight to thirty. They move in search of food, sometimes swimming across rivers and lakes to reach new pastures.

Below: Many children in the north adore their reindeer "pets." Northern peoples have long made use of the reindeer's agility on snow, by harnessing reindeer to sleighs. There is even a mobile dwelling built on runners and moved by reindeer.

A "Reindeer Culture"

The minorities in northern Russia consist of many different ethnic groups, including the Chukchi and the Yakut. Many of these groups are reindeer herders. The Chukchi are divided into two groups: the reindeer Chukchi, who live off their reindeer herds, and the maritime Chukchi, who survive by fishing and hunting in the Arctic Sea and along its coasts. The Yakut also breed cattle and horses; their diet consists mainly of fish and dairy products, with meat reserved for special occasions.

The harsh, cold climate of the north has given rise to a kind of "reindeer culture," where humans and reindeer depend on each other for survival. Reindeer are important to the people of the north because every part of the animal can be used for food, clothing, or making tools. Reindeer also produce small quantities of a rich, nourishing milk.

A Vanishing, Nomadic Lifestyle

Reindeer herders lead a nomadic lifestyle, moving the herd from place to place in search of lichens, shoots, and other vegetation. It is not unusual for a group of herders to travel up to 250 miles (400 km) a year. A typical group of herders may consist of two to seven families, or up to seventy people!

After the October Revolution, the Communist Party settled the Chukchi on collective farms and introduced new economic activities among them. Many Chukchi abandoned reindeer herding for agricultural jobs. Today, the Yakut continue to breed reindeer, but many families have settled on farms, adopting modern farming methods and equipment. Although these minority groups retain their distinct ethnic identities, their nomadic lifestyle is slowly vanishing as urbanization and industrialization increase in northern Russia.

Above: **A family of reindeer herders. Their dwellings are tents, which may be taken down when it is time to move, and set up again in the new pastures.**

The Siberian Tiger

Power and Beauty

The magnificent Siberian tiger is the largest cat species in the world. It grows to an average height of 3.5 feet (1.1 m) and may reach a length of 12 feet (3.6 m). The heaviest Siberian tiger on record was a hefty 845 pounds (384 kg)!

Although it is also found in northern China and Korea, the Siberian tiger inhabits mainly the eastern part of Siberia, the region along the Amur and Ussuri rivers. It lives by rocky streams, on cliffs, and in forests, surviving on a diet of large animals, such as deer, boar, and elk, as well as smaller creatures, such as rabbits and fish. The tiger stalks its prey, moving stealthily closer, until it pounces on the victim, grabbing it by the neck or throat and suffocating it. Hunting can be a long and tedious process for the tiger. Only about one in ten hunting trips is successful, especially when the tiger clashes with large animals, such as bear and elk. To cope with the cold, harsh climate, the

Below: **Siberian tigers in captivity. Scientists are trying to learn more about the tigers' habits. Since 1992, scientists have been capturing wild tigers and "tagging" them with radio collars. When these animals are released, scientists can track them through the signals emitted by the radio transmitters.**

Siberian tiger has several features unique to its species. For example, its coat is longer than that of its smaller, Asian counterpart, the Bengal tiger. In the winter, the light orange fur of the Siberian tiger takes on an even lighter color, to help camouflage it in the surrounding snow. The tiger also develops a layer of fat to insulate it against freezing temperatures.

Above: **The power and grace of the beautiful Siberian tiger. A fast runner, the tiger may chase its prey for a considerable distance before giving up.**

Conservation Efforts

Fewer than eight hundred of these beautiful animals survive in the world. Only about three hundred are wild. The main threat they face is the disappearance of their natural habitat as Siberia opens up to settlement, industrialization, agriculture, and other human activities. In 1992, the Law of the Russian Federation on Environmental Protection and Management prohibited the poaching of Siberian tigers. However, illegal hunting still decreases the wild tiger population every year. People prize the animals' beautiful coats, and some believe tiger bones have healing properties.

About five hundred Siberian tigers live in captivity in zoos all around the world. The Siberian Tiger Project is a joint effort by American and Russian scientists to study the behavior and needs of the Siberian tiger in the Russian Far East. With careful research and the preservation of the tigers' natural environment, humans may be able to reverse the harmful effects of their relationship with the tiger, before it is too late.

Valentina Tereshkova and the Space Program

The Soviet space program was one of the most advanced in the world during its time. Few people know that the first maps ever made of the far side of the moon (the side never visible from Earth) were drawn from information gathered by the Soviet space probe *Luna 3*. In 1957, the U.S.S.R. launched Earth's first artificial satellite, *Sputnik 1*. In 1959 alone, the U.S.S.R. launched three successful probes to the moon. Two years later, cosmonaut Yuri Gagarin became the first man in space. In the 1960s and 1970s, unmanned space probes to Venus and Mars followed.

Left: **A success of the Soviet space program, the Buran reusable orbital spaceship was launched in 1988.**

The Russian space program has not been without tragedies — three men died in an accident on *Soyuz 3* in 1971. But Russia went on to further achievements, including the orbiting space stations, *Salyut* and *Mir*. Today, Russia and the United States cooperate on space projects that have enriched both countries' programs.

Above: **Valentina Tereshkova, seen here at Heathrow Airport, England, in 1984. Beside her at the Concorde controls is Don Hullah, engineer of the aircraft.**

First Woman in Space

The U.S.S.R. was the first country to put a woman in space. In June, 1963, Valentina Tereshkova made a three-day flight in *Vostok 6*, orbiting Earth forty-eight times. Twice awarded the Order of Lenin, she also received one of the highest awards in the former Soviet Union, Hero of the U.S.S.R.

Valentina Tereshkova was born in 1937, in Masslenikovo, a small village north of Moscow. Her father was a tractor driver on a farm, and her mother worked in the textile industry. Tereshkova's first job was in a tire factory. As a youth, she was an active parachuting enthusiast in Komsomol, the Communist Youth Organization. Inspired by Yuri Gagarin's flight in 1961, Tereshkova joined the Cosmonaut Corps in 1962. She made history herself the following year when she orbited Earth.

Weekend at a Dacha

Many Russians who live in cities or towns also own houses in the countryside. A country house is called a *dacha* (DA-cha). Many dachas are simple wooden houses, but some belonging to successful businesspeople or important government officials may resemble grand palaces. Some dachas have been renovated or restored and converted into tourist attractions or small hotels.

Typically, a dacha functions as a weekend or holiday retreat, enabling people to get away from the hectic lifestyle and pollution of the big city. In the summer, an endless line of traffic heads out of Moscow on a Friday, as crowds of people leave the city for their countryside dachas!

A dacha is usually a two-story wooden house standing in its own private grounds. The living and dining rooms are downstairs, and there is often a small balcony upstairs. Outside the dacha, many families have a banya, or a private bath house. The banya is a wooden building resembling a sauna. Inside the

Below: **A Russian man stands proudly beside his dacha.**

Above: **The beautiful interior of a dacha, Leonid House.**

banya are benches for people to sit or lie on. Steam is produced by pouring water onto red-hot stones. Some people believe that steaming is a healthy, cleansing process that opens up the pores of the skin. In the banya, Russians use birch twigs as switches to swat themselves gently, easing the muscles and leaving a wonderful smell! Then, they take an invigorating dip in a pond, lake, or river. In winter, they sometimes even roll in the snow. The banya is as much a part of Russian life as the dacha. In the past, babies were born in the banya, and bodies washed there before burial.

Some families grow fruit and vegetables, or raise poultry and sheep on the land surrounding their dacha. This was more important in the past, when it was often difficult to obtain fresh food in the countryside. Many dachas serve as a home base for people picking mushrooms or going fishing, hunting, or boating in the surrounding countryside.

In the evenings, many Russians build a fire and cook shashlyk (lamb kebabs) over a birch bar and logs — the Russian version of a barbecue! Then, in the relaxing sunset, they enjoy the warmth of the fire and the company of family and friends.

Winter Fun

Much of Russia is inland, far from the warming influence of ocean currents. As a result, many regions, such as central Siberia and Yakutia, experience freezing winters. Adequate winter clothing is essential, especially to people living in northern Russia, close to the Arctic Circle. Possibly the coldest place in the world is near Verkhoyansk, in Yakutia, where a low of -96° F (-71° C) has been recorded. Even in western Russia, temperatures can fall below -40° F (-40° C).

In their leisure time, many Russians work on craft projects and pursue other indoor hobbies to keep themselves occupied, especially during winter. However, because winter is such a long season in many parts of their country, Russians have learned not to let the cold deter them. With suitable clothing and equipment, Russians enjoy all kinds of outdoor activities, from festive street processions to amateur and professional sports.

Below: **A Christmas procession in the snow.**

Above: **A cross-country skiing competition in Murmansk.**

Activities for Children

Like children in the West, Russian children love playing in the snow. They enjoy building snowmen, having snowball fights, tobogganing, and riding on snowmobiles. In the northern part of the country, some people travel in sleighs pulled by reindeer. There are even winter festivals where people parade in the snow-covered streets in colorful traditional costumes before sitting down to a hearty winter feast.

Snow Sports

Professional Russian athletes traditionally excel at winter sports such as ice skating, ice hockey, and skiing. The average Russian also enjoys these sports. When the ponds and lakes freeze over, children and adults alike put on their ice skates and take to the smooth, icy surface. The snowy slopes of the Caucasus Mountains are a popular choice with skiers. Because snow is plentiful here all year round, Russians can go skiing on this mountain range even in the summer. Skiing competitions draw crowds of enthusiasts every year. Moscow has ski-jumping facilities that remain open throughout the year. During the summer, a layer of synthetic material is used to simulate snow!

74

RELATIONS WITH NORTH AMERICA

Throughout much of its history, Russia remained a mystery to the rest of the world. The Viking grand princes' early efforts to connect Russia to Western Europe ended with the Mongol invasion in the thirteenth century. Even after the sixteenth century, when the tsars opened Russia up to trade with Western Europe, foreign perceptions of Russians were often unfavorable. Russians were frequently misunderstood and perceived as being uncivilized, barbaric, and brutal.

Opposite: **The Vostok rocket at the former Exhibition of Soviet Economic Achievements in Moscow.**

Below: **Russian immigrants on a sidewalk in New York.**

Contact between Russia and North America was limited before the twentieth century. After the October Revolution brought the communists to power, Russia closed its doors to the rest of the world. For more than sixty years, relations between the U.S.S.R. and North America were distorted by propaganda on both sides. In the United States, there was widespread fear of a communist threat and of Russian military aggression. In the U.S.S.R., politicians distrusted the West and strove to outdo its achievements. Friendly ties between Russia and North America are a relatively recent and very welcome development.

The Cold War

Relations with North America turned sour after World War II. During the war, the U.S.S.R. and the United States were allies, united against Germany. With their common enemy defeated, however, both sides discovered that their different government systems and ideals were incompatible. Each country also had a store of nuclear weapons, which sparked mutual suspicion and fear. The result was the Cold War, a nonviolent battle of words, threats, and political ideologies. A generation of Americans and Russians grew up under the constant threat of nuclear war. The

United States and the U.S.S.R. were the main players in a game that could wipe out humankind.

The Cold War heated up in 1948, when the Soviet Union blockaded the former German capital, Berlin. After World War II, Berlin was divided among France, Britain, the United States, and the U.S.S.R. In 1948, the Soviet Union cut off all road and rail links to the city; food and fuel could only be supplied by air. The Soviet government lifted the blockade when the Western powers refused to withdraw from Berlin. The damage, however, had been done — the United States considered the U.S.S.R. its enemy.

Above: **Joseph McCarthy irresponsibly fed American fears of the spread of communism in the United States.**

McCarthyism

In February 1950, an undistinguished U.S. senator achieved overnight fame by claiming that 205 communists had infiltrated the U.S. State Department. When a committee was set up to investigate his claim, Joseph McCarthy was unable to prove any of his accusations or name a single so-called communist. However, in the United States, there was already intense suspicion and hatred of Soviet expansion in Eastern Europe. McCarthy's groundless accusations ignited public opinion and led to the persecution of many innocent Americans. The senator's colleagues finally censured him publicly in 1954, ending the era of McCarthyism. American suspicion and dislike of the U.S.S.R. persisted, however, well into the 1960s and 1970s.

Left: **Throughout the 1960s and 1970s, suspicious American officials kept a close watch on Soviet activities and the movement of Soviet ships and aircraft. This photograph was taken by U.S. Air Force personnel. It shows missiles being shipped back to the U.S.S.R. from Cuba in 1962.**

The Division of Berlin and the Cuban Missile Crisis

The tension between the United States and the Soviet Union worsened in the years that followed. This was also an era of spy scandals, when every American and every Soviet was regarded by the other side as a potential spy.

In 1956, the U.S.S.R. invaded Hungary, to the anger of the United States. In 1961, Berlin once again became the focus of world attention when the Berlin Wall was built, dividing the city into two — one under communist rule, the other under Western rule. The United States discovered a year later, in 1962, that the Soviet Union had placed nuclear missiles in Cuba within range of major American cities. U.S. President John F. Kennedy ordered a full military alert and a naval blockade of Cuba, demanding that the missiles be removed. Fortunately, Soviet President Nikita Khrushchev backed down in time to avert war.

Above: **The United States and the U.S.S.R. were on opposite sides of many conflicts throughout the 1960s and 1970s, including the Vietnam War. Within the United States itself, opinion was divided. There were pro- and anti-war demonstrations outside the White House in Washington D. C. in the 1960s.**

Clashing Over World Affairs

For about twenty years, throughout the 1960s and 1970s, people considered two world powers stronger and more influential than any other — the U.S.S.R. and the United States. These two competing superpowers often intervened in the politics of other nations. In so doing, they risked further offending each other.

For example, when the United States entered the Vietnam War on the side of South Vietnam, Soviet–American relations worsened because communist North Vietnam had the military and political backing of the U.S.S.R.

The Arms Race and the Space Race

By the 1970s, both the United States and the U.S.S.R. were increasing their efforts at keeping peace. In 1967, the Outer Space Treaty prohibited both sides from placing nuclear weapons in space. The rivalry known as the space race had begun years earlier, when the Soviets became the first to send a man into space in 1961. In turn, the United States put the first man on the moon, astronaut Neil Armstrong. Both sides were competing to develop space weapons and new space technology. In 1968, the Treaty on the Non-Proliferation of Nuclear Weapons helped slow down the arms race, the rivalry between the two powers over weapons.

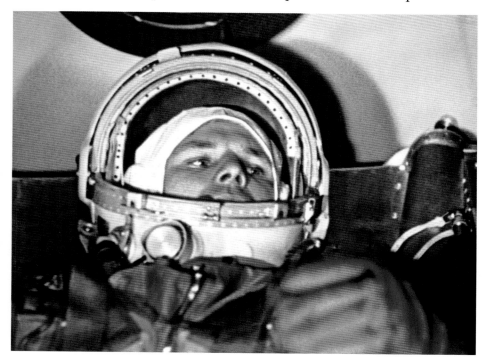

Left: **Soviet cosmonaut Yuri Gagarin became the first man in space in 1961, sparking a scramble between the United States and the U.S.S.R. for superiority in space research and achievements.**

Forging a Strong Friendship

Despite disagreements over military action, especially in Vietnam, the United States and Russia have drawn closer in recent years, especially after the dissolution of the U.S.S.R. in 1991 and the dismantling of the Berlin Wall. Much of the new harmony between Russia and North America began with improved ties between former Soviet president Mikhail Gorbachev and former U.S. presidents Ronald Reagan and George Bush. Today, Russian president Boris Yeltsin and U.S. president Bill Clinton are preserving these warm relations. Scientists in both countries are cooperating on joint conservation efforts, including the Siberian Tiger Project. American and Russian scientists have also worked together on board the Russian space station *Mir*, which translates, appropriately, into "world," as well as "peace." Four hundred years of conflict and distrust have come to a timely end.

Below: **Soviet and American leaders in 1985 in Geneva, Switzerland. Warm ties established by former Soviet president Mikhail Gorbachev and then U.S. president Ronald Reagan were continued by President George Bush and now, Presidents Bill Clinton and Boris Yeltsin.**

Immigration

There have been several waves of immigration from Russia to the West, particularly to the United States and Canada. During the nineteenth and early twentieth centuries, many Jewish people fled Russia to escape religious persecution. In brutal attacks called *pogroms* (poh-GROMMS), troops ravaged Jewish settlements in Ukraine. In 1905, there was a rebellion against Tsar Nicholas II. The tsar, wrongly convinced that the uprising had been a Jewish plot to overthrow him, intensified persecution of Russian Jews. Many found refuge in North America.

The 1917 October Revolution and the terrible civil war that followed led to other groups leaving Russia. Fearing the communist government and the loss not only of their riches but also their lives, many Russian nobles fled to parts of the Black Sea, sailing to France and Great Britain. Some then went on to North America. After World War II, many Ukrainians and Cossacks who had fought on Germany's side during the war preferred to remain abroad rather than return to Stalin's regime. Many Ukrainians settled on farms in the Canadian provinces of Manitoba, Saskatchewan, and Alberta. Since 1991, many Russians have also emigrated to the West in search of new lives.

Above: **Jewish immigrants of Russian and Polish origin in New York in the 1890s. During the nineteenth and early twentieth centuries, many Jewish people fled brutal killings in what is today Ukraine.**

81

Russians in North America

During the Soviet era, many intellectuals and artists fled the U.S.S.R. for a better life in Western Europe and North America. Russian novelist and historian Alexander Solzhenitsyn (1918–) was exiled from the Soviet Union in 1974, after years of imprisonment and the censorship of his writing. He settled on an estate in Cavendish, Vermont, in the United States. During his twenty-year exile, Solzhenitsyn published several books on Russian relations with the United States. In 1970, he was awarded the Nobel Prize for Literature. Solzhenitsyn's influential works include *One Day in the Life of Ivan Denisovich* (1962), *August* (1971), and *The Gulag Archipelago* (1973), the work that got him exiled.

The U.S.S.R. also lost many talented ballet stars to the West. Rudolf Nureyev (1938–1993), Natalia Makarova (1940–), and Mikhail Baryshnikov (1948–), considered three of ballet's greats, all chose to remain in the West while touring with Russian ballet companies. Makarova joined the American Ballet Theater in New York, shortly after leaving the Kirov Ballet in 1970. Nureyev made his American debut in 1962 and made numerous television and stage appearances. Baryshnikov joined the American Ballet Theater in 1974 and has also ventured into acting.

Above: **Alexander Solzhenitsyn.**

Below: **The remarkable dance partnership of Rudolf Nureyev and Margot Fonteyn (1919–1991). Although he never signed on permanently with any dance company in the West, Nureyev was a guest performer with the Royal Ballet in London, England.**

North Americans in Russia

Before 1991, all foreigners had to have the permission of the
Soviet government to work or live in Russia. Businessman
Armand Hammer was one of the few Americans trusted by
the Soviet regime. He helped donate funds to the U.S.S.R.
during periods of famine, and also after the nuclear accident
at Chernobyl.

Today, foreign professionals from all over the world visit or
live in Russia, advising the government or running private
enterprises. Canadian technicians have been helping in the oil
and gas industries in the Russian far north, while Americans have
been assisting steel production and the re-organization of the
Hermitage Museum in St. Petersburg. In 1997, an American
astronaut assisted in repairs after an explosion damaged part of
the Russian space station *Mir*. North American investment and
special intelligence operations are also helping to combat social
problems such as organized crime, drug smuggling, and arms
trafficking in Russia.

Above: **An American
business mission to
St. Petersburg. Many
North American
investors see big-
business opportunities
in Russia.**

Left: Tsar Nicholas II and his family before the October Revolution in 1917. When Lenin and the Bolsheviks rose to power, Nicholas and his entire family were killed in 1918, with Anastasia *(extreme right)* probably among them. But because not all the remains could be identified, people continued to speculate about Anastasia's possible survival.

Anastasia: the Original and the Imposters

One Russian historical figure has a special place in the American imagination — Anastasia. The real Anastasia was born near St. Petersburg in 1901. The youngest daughter of Nicholas II, the last of the tsars, Anastasia probably died with the rest of her family when they were murdered by the Bolsheviks. However, there is no concrete evidence that she died. American fascination with the possibility of Anastasia's survival reached new heights in the 1960s, when a woman calling herself Anna Anderson claimed to be the real Anastasia. Anderson married an American in 1968 and lived in the United States until her death in 1984. She was by no means the first person to assume Anastasia's identity, but she became the most famous when she tried to establish herself as the legal heir to the Romanov fortune held in Swiss banks. In 1970, West German courts finally rejected her claim. DNA tests have recently confirmed that Anderson was really a woman of Polish and German origin, Franzisca Schanzkowska.

ANASTASIA: THE MOVIES

In 1956, Hollywood produced the film *Anastasia*, based on a French play of the same title written by Marcel-Maurette two years earlier. Famous actress Ingrid Bergman won an Academy Award for playing the Russian princess. Anastasia continues to intrigue filmmakers today. Her story received its latest revival in the 1997 animated film, *Anastasia*, with American actress Meg Ryan lending her voice to the title role.

Come to the Circus!

The circus as we know it — with clowns, acrobats, trainers, and animal performers — began in England in the eighteenth century as a much simpler horseback riding performance. As new acts were added, the circus grew in size and popularity.

A man named Charles Hughes introduced the circus to Russia in the eighteenth century. He had originally been asked to deliver some horses to Catherine the Great. To impress the empress, he included a company of riders who could perform tricks on horseback. Catherine was so pleased that she gave Hughes a private circus in the royal palace in St. Petersburg.

Today, the most famous Russian circus is the Moscow Circus, which has toured in North America and Europe. The great Russian clown Oleg Popov shot to fame through his hilarious circus performances with this troupe. In Russia, the circus is regarded as a valuable art form, and the state invests a lot of money in promoting it. The Moscow Circus performs in a permanent building in Moscow — an indoor theater with separate rings for water and ice shows!

Below: **A performer with the Moscow Circus rides around the ring waving a long banner with the Russian colors.**

RUSSIA

	A	B	C	D
1				
2				
3				
4				
5				

State Boundary
Capital
City
River
Republic Boundary
16 Republic

ARCTIC OCEAN

BARENTS SEA

SEVERNAYA ZEMLYA

NEW S ISL

SWEDEN

FINLAND

● Murmansk

NOVAYA ZEMLYA

BALTIC SEA

ESTONIA

● Kaliningrad

LATVIA

LITHUANIA

BELARUS

● St. Petersburg

Novgorod

● Arkhangelsk

Central Siberian Plateau

SIBERIA

21

● Yaroslavl

■ MOSCOW

● Ivanovo

West Siberian Plain

URAL MOUNTAINS

Ob

Yenisey

● Chernobyl
Kiev

UKRAINE

Central Russian Upland

Don

10 11

9

● Kazan

12

13

Volga

14

● Samara

● Yekaterinburg

● Tobolsk

Irtysh

15

BLACK SEA

Mt. Elbrus
(18,510 feet/
5,640 m)

● Astrakhan

CAUCASUS

GEORGIA

ARMENIA

AZERBAIJAN

CASPIAN SEA

1

2

3

5

6

7

8

● Novosibirsk

Lake Baykal

18

● Irkutsk

20

● Ulan Ude

Chi

19

17

KAZAKHSTAN

TURKMENISTAN

UZBEKISTAN

KYRGYZSTAN

CHINA

MONGOLIA

TAJIKISTAN

86

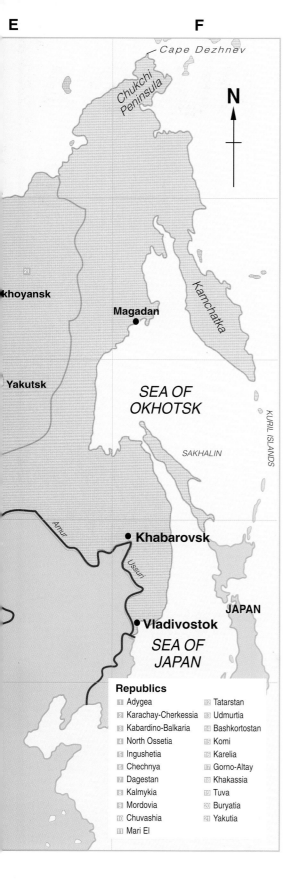

E **F**

Cape Dezhnev

Chukchi Peninsula

N

khoyansk

Magadan

Kamchatka

Yakutsk

SEA OF OKHOTSK

SAKHALIN

KURIL ISLANDS

Amur

Ussuri

● **Khabarovsk**

JAPAN

● **Vladivostok**

SEA OF JAPAN

Republics	
① Adygea	⑫ Tatarstan
② Karachay-Cherkessia	⑬ Udmurtia
③ Kabardino-Balkaria	⑭ Bashkortostan
④ North Ossetia	⑮ Komi
⑤ Ingushetia	⑯ Karelia
⑥ Chechnya	⑰ Gorno-Altay
⑦ Dagestan	⑱ Khakassia
⑧ Kalmykia	⑲ Tuva
⑨ Mordovia	⑳ Buryatia
⑩ Chuvashia	㉑ Yakutia
⑪ Mari El	

Amur River E4
Arctic Ocean A1–F1
Arkhangelsk B2
Armenia A4
Astrakhan A4
Azerbaijan A4

Baltic Sea A2
Barents Sea B1–C1
Baykal, Lake D4
Belarus A2
Black Sea A4

Caspian Sea A4
Caucasus Mountains A4
Central Russian Upland A3
Central Siberian Plateau D2
Chernobyl A3
China C5–E4
Chita D4
Chukchi Peninsula F1

Dezhnev, Cape F1
Don River A3

Estonia A2

Finland A2–B1

Georgia A4

Irkutsk D4
Irtysh River C3
Ivanovo A2

Japan F4

Kaliningrad A2
Kamchatka Peninsula F2
Kazakhstan B4
Kazan B3
Khabarovsk F4
Kiev (Ukraine) A3
Kuril Islands F3
Kyrgyzstan B5

Latvia A2
Lena River E2
Lithuania A2

Magadan F2
Mongolia D4
Moscow A2
Murmansk B2
Mt. Elbrus A4

New Siberian Islands D1
Novaya Zemlya C2
Novgorod A2
Novosibirsk C4

Ob River C3

Sakhalin Island F3
Samara B3
Sea of Japan F4
Sea of Okhotsk F3
Severnaya Zemlya D1
Siberia (region) D3
St. Petersburg A2
Sweden A1

Tajikistan B5
Tobolsk B3
Turkmenistan A4–B5

Ukraine A2–A3
Ulan Ude D4
Ural Mountains B3
Ussuri River F4
Uzbekistan A4–B5

Verkhoyansk E2
Vladivostok F4
Volga River B3

West Siberian Plain C3

Yakutsk E3
Yaroslavl A2
Yekaterinburg B3
Yenisey River C3

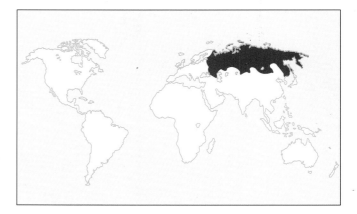

RUSSIA

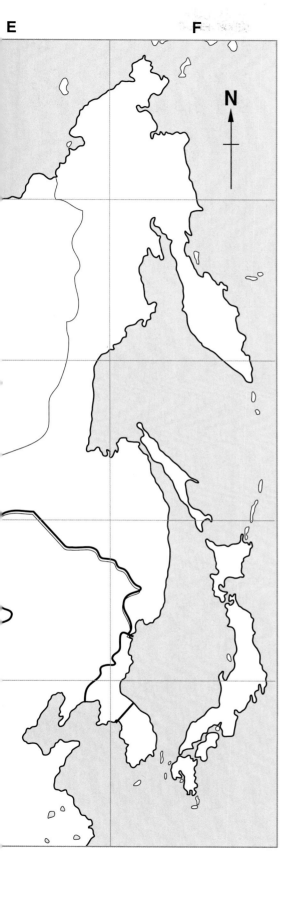

How Is Your Geography?

Learning to identify the main geographical areas and points of a country can be challenging. Although it may seem difficult at first to memorize the location and spelling of major cities or the names of mountain ranges, rivers, deserts, lakes, and other prominent physical features, the end result of this effort can be very rewarding. Places you previously did not know existed will suddenly come to life when referred to in world news, whether in newspapers, television reports, or other books and reference sources. This knowledge will make you feel a bit closer to the rest of the world, with its fascinating variety of cultures and physical geography.

For use in a classroom setting, the instructor can make duplicates of this map using a copy machine (PLEASE DO NOT WRITE IN THIS BOOK!). Students can then fill in any requested information on their individual map copies. For use one-on-one, the student can also make copies of the map on a copy machine and use them as a study tool. The student can practice identifying place names and geographical features on his or her own.

Russia at a Glance

Official Name   Russia; the Russian Federation

Capital   Moscow

Official Language   Russian

Population   1.5 million (1998 estimate)

Land Area   6.6 million square miles (17.1 million square km)

Republics   Adygea, Bashkortostan, Buryatia, Chechnya, Chuvashia, Dagestan, Gorno-Altay, Ingushetia, Kabardino-Balkaria, Kalmykia, Karachay-Cherkessia, Karelia, Khakassia, Komi, Mari El, Mordovia, North Ossetia, Tatarstan, Tuva, Udmurtia, Yakutia

Highest Point   Mt. Elbrus (18,510 feet / 5,640 m)

Major Rivers   Ob (3,362 miles / 5,410 km including the Irtysh)

Yenisey (2,540 miles / 4,090 km)

Volga (2,193 miles / 3,530 km)

Don (1,160 miles / 1,870 km)

Major Religion   Russian Orthodox Church

Famous Leaders   Peter the Great (1672–1725)

Catherine the Great (1729–1796)

Vladimir Lenin (1870–1924)

Joseph Stalin (1879–1953)

Mikhail Gorbachev (1931–)

Current President   Boris Yeltsin (1931–)

Important Holidays   New Year (January 1)

Orthodox Christmas (January 7)

National Day (June 12)

Currency   Ruble (6.06 rubles = U.S. $1 as of 1998)

Opposite: **A giant Soviet mural on a wall in Palace Square, St. Petersburg.**

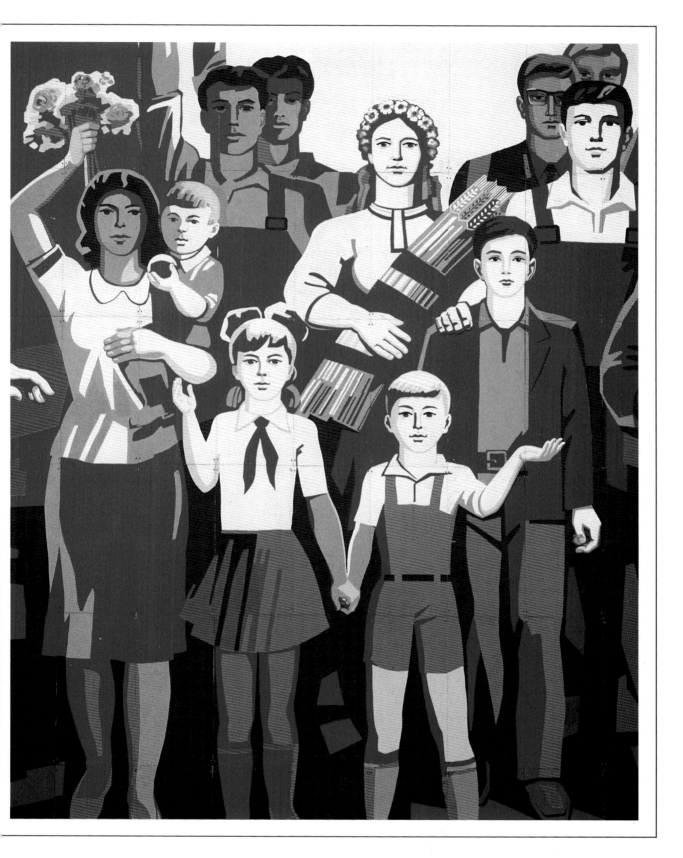

Glossary

Russian Words

babushki (ba-BOOSH-kee): grandmothers.

balalaika (bal-al-AI-ka): triangular stringed instrument played like a guitar.

banya (BAN-ya): a traditional Russian steam bath.

besprisorniki (bes-pree-ZORN-ikee): neglected children from families broken by divorce or separation.

bliny (BLEE-nye): pancakes.

borshch (BORSH): Russian soup made of beets and other vegetables.

chastushka (chahs-TOOSH-ka): a four-line verse set to music.

Cheka (CHEK-a): secret police force set up by Lenin.

dacha (DA-cha): country house.

glasnost (GLAHS-nohst): openness.

grozny (GROHZ-nye): awe-inspiring; formidable.

izba (IZ-ba): wooden houses in the Russian countryside.

matriyoshki (ma-tree-OSH-kee): Russian nesting dolls.

Oprichniki (ah-PREECH-ni-kee): black-robed horsemen, the secret police of Ivan the Terrible.

pelmeni (PEL-me-nee): Russian ravioli; small pieces of meat wrapped in flour.

perestroika (pe-res-STROY-ka): restructuring.

pogroms (poh-GROMMS): large scale murders of Jews in the nineteenth and early twentieth centuries.

samovary (SAM-o-VAR-ree): metal tea urns.

shashlyk (shash-LIK): lamb kebabs.

smetana (SMET-ana): sour cream.

solyanka (sol-YAN-ka): thick broth of meat and vegetables.

troika (TROY-ka): Russian carriage, sleigh, or wagon pulled by three horses abreast; a team of three horses driven abreast.

zakuski (ZAK-oos-kee): appetizers.

English Vocabulary

abdicate: to give up authority or an official position in a formal way.

autonomous: self-governing.

avid: eager.

blockade: to close off a place, usually by hostile ships or troops, and prevent entry and exit.

camouflage: to disguise or conceal by blending into the surroundings.

capitalism: an economic system in which individuals and groups invest in and own enterprises, with the least possible government intervention.

collectivization: a system implemented by Lenin's government, in which farms were organized into large units to gather and redistribute crop yields.

communism: theory or system of social organization based on common ownership of property and equality of the people first written about by German political philosopher Karl Marx.

conservative: tending to preserve existing conditions or restore traditional ones, and to limit change.

constitution: the system of basic principles according to which a country is governed.

cosmonaut: a Soviet or Russian astronaut.

cuisine: a style or way of cooking, usually belonging to a certain culture or country.

defect (v): to leave a country or a cause for political reasons.

denomination: branch of a certain religion.

eccentric: unusual; peculiar; moving away from the accepted or regular methods or attitudes.

effigy: image or model of something or someone.

extracurricular: outside the regular program of courses.

formidable: causing fear or inspiring awe.

hibernate: to spend the winter sleeping.

infrastructure: all of the facilities serving a country, area, or industry.

initiative: readiness and ability to take independent action.

insulate: to protect or cover, usually with a layer of material or fat.

intermarriage: marriage between persons of two different ethnic, cultural, or racial backgrounds.

legacy: something that is handed down from the past.

market economy: an economy where prices are determined by the forces of demand and supply.

mascot: an animal, person, or object adopted by a group as its symbol and source of good luck.

modernize: to make new or bring up-to-date, and to improve through such a change.

pagan: follower of a religion that has many gods.

paralyze: to make someone powerless or unable to act.

privatization: the process of transferring state-owned enterprises to individuals and groups.

propaganda: information or ideas that are deliberately spread to promote or harm a certain cause, movement, or country.

proportional representation: a method of voting that gives political parties legislative representation according to the relative popular vote earned. The more votes earned by a party, the greater that party's representation in government.

rabbinical: having to do with Jewish laws, learning, or writings.

radiation sickness: a sickness caused by overexposure to X-rays and dangerous energy rays.

radical: favoring extensive political, economic, or social reforms.

regime: a system of government; the government that is in power.

republic: a state in which supreme power rests in a body of citizens entitled to vote.

stereotype: an oversimplified, often incorrect, image or idea of a person or group.

turbine: a machine with blades that are driven by steam, water, hot gases, or air.

tyranny: the unrestrained use of power and abuse of authority.

vandalize: to deliberately destroy or damage private or public property.

More Books to Read

Boris Yeltsin and the Rebirth of Russia. Steven Otfinoski (The Millbrook Press)

Chagall. Masters of Art series. Gianni Pozzi, Claudia Saraceni, and L. R. Galante (Peter Bedrick)

The Empire of the Czars. Esther Carrion (Children's Press)

The New Russia. John Gillies (Macmillan)

Russia. Cultures of the World series. Oleg Torchinsky (Marshall Cavendish)

Russia. Festivals of the World series. Harlinah Whyte (Gareth Stevens)

Russia. Through the Eyes of Children series. Connie Bickman (Abdo Consulting Group)

Russia: Building Democracy. Topics in the News series. John Bradley (Raintree Steck-Vaughn)

Russia: New Freedoms, New Challenges. Exploring Cultures of the World series. Virginia Schomp (Marshall Cavendish)

Russian Americans. Cultures of America series. Steven Ferry (Marshall Cavendish)

Russian Girl: Life in an Old Russian Town. Russ Kendall (Scholastic)

Videos

Moscow and Leningrad: the Crown Jewels of Russia. (International Video Network)

Peter the Great. (Starmaker, an imprint of National Broadcasting Corporation)

Russia: Discovering Russia. (International Video Network)

Russia Then and Now. (Clay Francisco Films)

Web Sites

www.valley.net/~transnat/

www.bucknell.edu/departments/russian/index.html

www.learner.org/exhibits/russia/intro.html

Due to the dynamic nature of the Internet, some web sites stay current longer than others. To find additional web sites, use a reliable search engine with one or more of the following keywords to help you locate information about Russia. Keywords: *Cossacks, Ivan the Terrible, Moscow, Russia, Russians, tsars, Boris Yeltsin.*

Index